Jesus, God's Gift of Love

ILLUSTRATED BY JIM PADGETT

Copyright © 1998 by Abingdon Press
Art copyright © 1994 and 1996 by Cokesbury

ISBN 0-687-08449-0

Abingdon Press

Manufactured in Singapore

98 99 00 01 02 03 04 05 06 07 – 10 9 8 7 6 5 4 3 2 1

Great Joy

Sweep, sweep, went the broom.
    An angel came to Mary's room.
    "Peace to you! Don't be afraid!
You know the promise God has made.

    You will have a baby boy.
He will bring the world great joy!"

Zzzzz, zzzz, Joseph slept.
    Into his dream the angel crept.
    "Joseph, don't you be afraid,
You know the promise God has made.

    Mary will have a baby boy.
He will bring the world great joy."

Elizabeth Crocker
Based on Luke 1:26-35; Matthew 1:18-24
Copyright © 1995 Cokesbury

You are to name him Jesus.

Matthew 1:21

Mary Rode a Donkey

Mary rode a donkey
All the way to Bethlehem.

A little grey donkey,
All the way to Bethlehem.

Joseph walked beside them
All the way to Bethlehem.

Down the dusty dirt road,
All the way to Bethlehem.

Gonna have a baby
When they get to Bethlehem.

When will they get there?
All the way to Bethlehem.

Long, long way to Bethlehem.
Long, long way to Bethlehem.

Elizabeth Crocker
Based on Luke 2:1-5
Copyright © 1996 Cokesbury

He went to be registered with Mary.

Luke 2:5

Baby Jesus Is Born

Walk! Walk! Walk!
Mary and Joseph walked to Bethlehem.
They were tired and wanted to rest.

Knock! Knock! Knock!
Joseph knocked on the door of the inn.
"May we sleep here tonight?" asked Joseph.

No! No! NO!
"I'm sorry," said the innkeeper. "I have no more room."

Turn! Turn! Turn!
Sadly, Mary and Joseph turned to walk away.

Wait! Wait! Wait!
"You may sleep in the stable," said the innkeeper.
"You will be warm with the animals."

Sleep! Sleep Sleep!
Mary and Joseph slept on the fresh straw.

Waa! Waa! Waa!
The baby Jesus cried
as Mary wrapped him in a soft blanket.

Shh! Shh! Shh!
Mary rocked the baby Jesus to sleep.

Sing! Sing! Sing!
The angels sang the good news that Jesus was born.

Daphna Flegal
Based on Luke 2
Copyright © 1990 Graded Press

She wrapped him in bands of cloth,
and laid him in a manger.

Luke 2:7 (Adapted)

Five Little Shepherds

Five little shepherds watching their sheep.
The first one said, "It's time to sleep."

The second one said, "Wait, do you see that light?'
The third one said, "It shines very bright!"

The fourth one said, "I hear angels sing."
The fifth one said, "Let's go see the tiny king."

Five little shepherds hurried on their way
To see baby Jesus born this day.

Daphna Flegal
Based on Luke 2:8-20

So they went with haste
and found Mary and Joseph,
and the child lying in the manger.

Luke 2: 16

Good News, Shepherds!

The shepherds found that crowded inn
And stable with the child within.

They knelt before the tiny babe
That God had sent to earth this day.

They shared with Mary all that they'd heard;
They repeated each of the angels' words.

Then through the town they spread the story
Of the angels' message and of all the glory.

Praise God for the Savior's birth,
And peace to all upon the earth.

Raney K. Good
Based on Luke 2:7-20
Copyright © 1998 Cokesbury

I am bringing you good news
of great joy for all the people.

Luke 2:10

Three Wise Men

Three wise men traveled far,
Following a big, bright star.

The first one said, "Look how it glows!"
The second one said, "Look where it goes!"

The third one said, "It shines so bright;
I know we'll find the king tonight!"

Three wise men traveled far,
Following a big, bright star.

There, ahead of them,
went the star.

Matthew 2:9

Wise Men Visit Jesus

Harumph! Harumph!
The wise men rode their camels
And followed the star.

Harumph! Harumph!
The wise men rode their camels
To find the new king.

Harumph! Harumph!
The wise men rode their camels
To Bethlehem.

"Look, the star has stopped!
Let's go into the house!"

The wise men knelt near Jesus
And gave him their gifts
Of gold, and myrrh, and frankincense.

Jesus was the new king!

Based on Matthew 2:1-11
Copyright © 1994 Cokesbury
Adapted

Opening their treasure chests,
they offered him gifts
of gold, frankincense, and myrrh.

Matthew 2:11

A Christmas Prayer

Thank you for the stable, safe and strong.
Thank you for Mary, Joseph, and the
    angels' song.
Thank you for the animals gathered there.
Thank you for the shepherds' prayer.
Thank you for the star above.
Thank you for Jesus, God's gift of love.